Round Up! 🐤 W9-DIV-485

Do you have your eagle eye ready? Search through this puzzle pad and see if you can round up the answers to these three activities. Good *cluck*! Best *fishes*!

Rabbits or Monkeys?

Are there more hidden carrots or bananas?

Fish Fun!

Can you spot all 6 hidden fish?

Snail Trail!

Can you find each of these hidden animals?

snail   bat   duck   caterpillar   butterfly

Cover illustrated by Dave Klug
Silly stories written by Betsy Ochester

Hidden Pictures®

Write a number below each object based on the order in which you find it in the big picture. Then flip the page to create a silly story with the objects!

carrot

pencil

umbrella

boot

anchor

eyeglasses

bird

teacup

fish

comb

bell

sailboat

Kitten Cuddles

Illustrated by Dave Klug

Flip the page!

Kitten Cuddles

Write the object names in the numbered spaces. For example, if you found the umbrella first, write "umbrella" in the first blank.

A couple of weeks ago, my fluffy calico

_____ had a litter of kittens. At first, they
     1

couldn't open their eyes or move out of their comfy

_____. My sister picked one up and said
     2

it looked just like a tiny, fuzzy _____!
                                3

Now they are big enough to play with us, and, boy,

does that make my _____ happy! They
                    4

love to chase string, table-tennis balls, and of course

that big fluffy _____ from the bookshelf.
                 5

Today was zany! As soon as we got home from

school, we raced to the _____. The
6

kittens came running and all seven of them leaped

right at my _____. Then the smallest
7

one batted a toy _____ from my sister's
8

_____ and onto the couch. My mom
9

came in and sat right on it. She jumped up faster

than a young _____ on a bouncy
10

_____. We all had a good laugh—even
11

Mom. I can't wait to see what happens tomorrow

when my best _____ comes over to play!
12

Hidden Pictures®

Write a number below each object based on the order in which you find it in the big picture. Then flip the page to create a silly story with the objects!

clothespin
○

banana
○

cactus
○

sock
○

watermelon
○

hat
○

paintbrush
○

pencil
○

bell
○

boot
○

candle
○

baseball
○

BONUS
Can you also find these objects?

iron

trowel

Big Fish

Illustrated by Patrick Girouard

Flip the page!

Big Fish

Write the object names in the numbered spaces. For example, if you found the cactus first, write "cactus" in the first blank.

Yesterday, our teacher had a big surprise for

us. We were going on a field trip to the new

_____! I'd wanted to go there ever
      1

since my _____ told me about it.
              2

It was just as great as I had imagined. I've seen

a _____ in a bowl before, but I've
        3

never seen so many at once. I felt like a little

_____ under the sea, swimming with
        4

a great white _____ and a striped
                    5

_____. My favorite part of the trip was
      6

when we saw a scientist put on a _____

7

and then dive right into a giant tank filled with a

special kind of _____. The scientist gave

8

the fish a _____ to eat, and then he took

9

photos. I think he might have even snapped one

through the water of me and my _____!

10

When I got home, I told my dad all about my trip,

especially the electric jumping _____. He

11

said that he'd like to see that, too. So we are going to

visit the _____ this weekend!

12

Hidden Pictures®

Write a number below each object based on the order in which you find it in the big picture. Then flip the page to create a silly story with the objects!

ring
◯

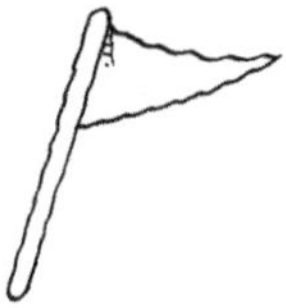

flag
◯

paintbrush
◯

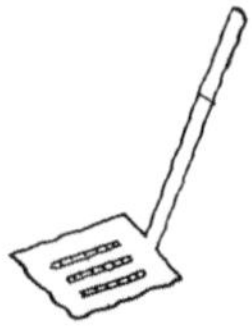

spatula
◯

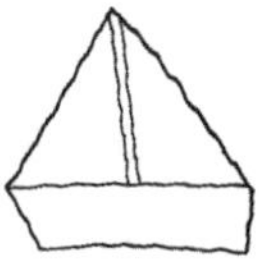

sailboat
◯

pencil
◯

kite
◯

magnifying glass
◯

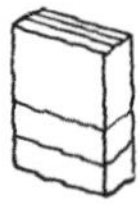

book
◯

crown
◯

ice-cream cone
◯

button
◯

BONUS
Can you also find this object?

tack

Bug Band

Illustrated by David Helton

Flip the page!

Bug Band

Write the object names in the numbered spaces. For example, if you found the sailboat first, write "sailboat" in the first blank.

The best _____ in the entire town of
　　　　　　　　1

_____ Valley is on stage. Barry Bug is
　　　2

the lead singer. He sings high notes that could shatter

a glass _____! But the drummer is my
　　　　　　　3

favorite _____ in the band. I once saw
　　　　　　4

him throw his _____ in the air, catch it
　　　　　　　　5

with one _____, and keep on playing.
　　　　　6

It was amazing! I want to learn to do that someday.

I think half the town showed up today. Some bugs

are eating _____ lunches. Some are
　　　　　　　7

lying on the _____ and enjoying the
8

music. Just as the band started playing their hit song,

"Row, Row, Row Your _____," a dark
9

_____ appeared above us and it started
10

to pour. Every bug was soaked to the wings! But the

band kept playing. I grabbed by friend, Mary Jo

_____, and we danced the jitterbug. It
11

was the best—and the wettest—_____
12

ever.

Hidden Pictures®

Write a number below each object based on the order in which you find it in the big picture. Then flip the page to create a silly story with the objects!

magnet
◯

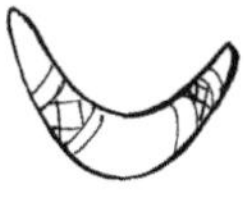

boomerang
◯

mallet
◯

sailboat
◯

cupcake
◯

bandage
◯

lollipop
◯

teacup
◯

feather
◯

thread
◯

spoon
◯

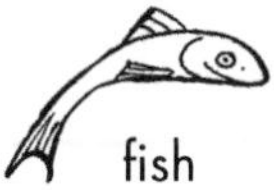

fish
◯

BONUS
Can you also find these objects?

 cane

 heart

 arrow

crescent moon

 musical note

 butterfly

Monkeyshines

Illustrated by Rocky Fuller

Flip the page!

Monkeyshines

Write the object names in the numbered spaces. For example, if you found the boomerang first, write "boomerang" in the first blank.

Most people don't know this, but monkeys love to

play board games. I learned this on my trip to the

country of West _____. While I was

               1

hiking through a thick _____, far away

               2

from the nearest _____, I heard strange

               3

noises, like someone rolling dice. I scratched my

_____. I was in the middle of nowhere.

               4

How could that be? Then I walked around a large

_____, and I saw them: four monkeys

               5

playing a board game, taking turns moving a

_____ around a _____!
          6   7

I was so surprised, you could have knocked me

over with a fluffy _____. My fingers
                                              8

trembled as I pulled my _____ from my
                                              9

backpack and started filming them. One was happily

munching on a _____, while another
                                        10

rolled the _____. Finally, one reached
                              11

the finish. He jumped up and down and waved a

_____ in triumph. It sure was something
          12

to see!

Hidden Pictures®

Write a number below each object based on the order in which you find it in the big picture. Then flip the page to create a silly story with the objects!

fried egg

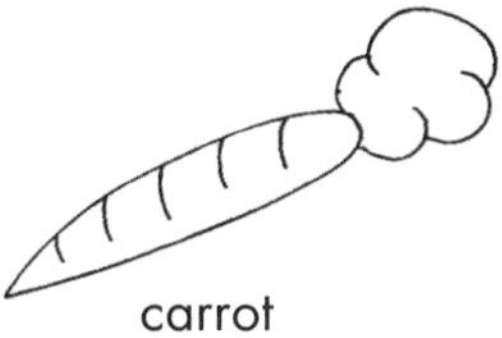

carrot

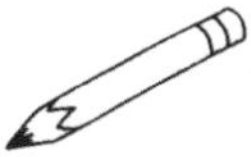

pencil

snow cone

ring

cupcake

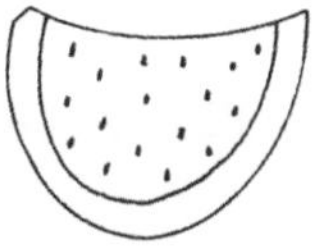

watermelon

hat

mitten

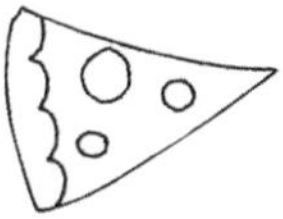

pizza

spoon

crown

BONUS
Can you find these objects?

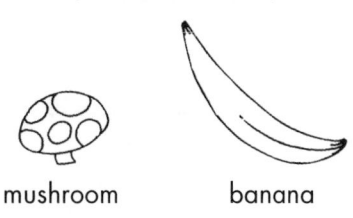

mushroom

banana

Surf's Up!

Flip the page!

Illustrated by Marilee Harrald-Pilz

Surf's Up!

Write the object names in the numbered spaces. For example, if you found the carrot first, write "carrot" in the first blank.

Today I saw something strange. My family was

taking a trip to the beach, and as I jumped

into the ocean, I looked up and saw a green

alligator riding a _____. He looked

1

like he was having a fabulous time, and so did his

friend, a little _____ with a polka-

2

dotted _____. I rubbed my eyes,

3

thinking I must be daydreaming. But it was no

_____—they were really there in the

4

warm, wavy _____. The alligator was

5

wearing a flowered _____ and had a
6

great big _____ on his face. He looked
7

so happy on his _____, just riding the
8

waves. It made me want to learn to surf, too. So I

asked my _____ if I could take some
9

lessons, and she said I could! I put on a waterproof

_____ and my best _____,
10   11

and my mom rented me a shiny, colorful

_____. I can't wait to hit the waves!
12

Hidden Pictures®

Write a number below each object based on the order in which you find it in the big picture. Then flip the page to create a silly story with the objects!

boot ◯

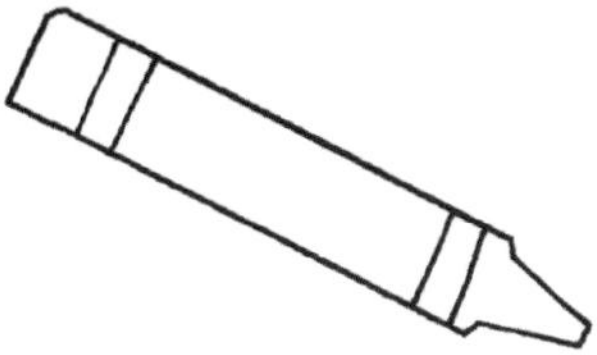

crayon ◯

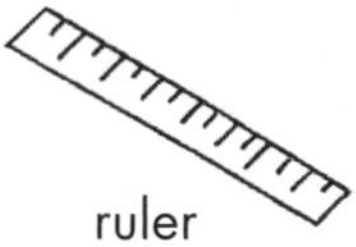

ruler ◯

candle ◯

purse ◯

crown ◯

bat ◯

sneaker ◯

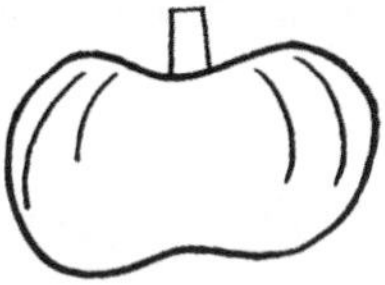

pumpkin ◯

pencil ◯

toothbrush ◯

megaphone ◯

BONUS
Can you find these objects?

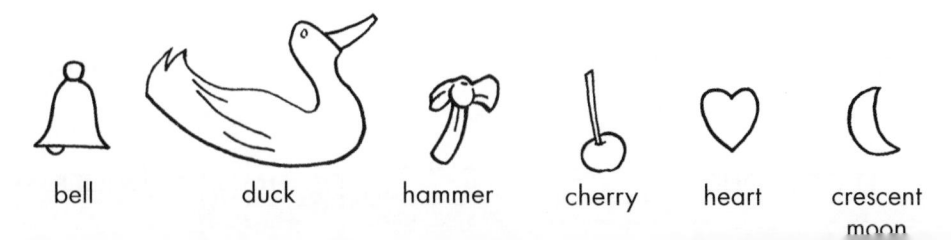

bell   duck   hammer   cherry   heart   crescent moon

Bunny Bakery

Illustrated by Mike DeSantis

Flip the page!

Bunny Bakery

Write the object names in the numbered spaces. For example, if you found the crayon first, write "crayon" in the first blank.

The Hopping _____ Bakery offers

1

the best carrot cake, _____ cookies,

2

and sweet _____ bread that money

3

can buy. The bakery has only been open for a

year, yet these hardworking bunnies have already

won the hearts—and stomachs—of everyone in

_____ City. The talented owner first

4

learned to bake by mixing up a _____

5

with a _____ and calling it Whipped

6

_____ Delight. Today his specialty is

7

creating the perfect four-layer _____
8

to enjoy at weddings. Some people are surprised to

learn that a little furry _____ can create
9

such treats. But it's true. Once a customer tastes the

chocolate _____ or samples just a lick
10

of a powdered _____, they learn the
11

truth about bunnies. They can bake better than any

_____ out there. Stop by today!
12

Hidden Pictures®

Write a number below each object based on the order in which you find it in the big picture. Then flip the page to create a silly story with the objects!

thread
◯

cane
◯

sailboat
◯

pencil
◯

glove
◯

crescent moon
◯

bananas
◯

musical note
◯

spoon
◯

magnet
◯

computer
◯

can opener
◯

BONUS
Can you also find this object?

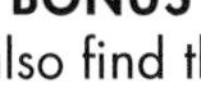

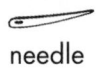

needle

Bird's-Eye View

Illustrated by Rocky Fuller

Flip the page!

Bird's-Eye View

Write the object names in the numbered spaces. For example, if you found the bananas first, write "bananas" in the first blank.

My name is Ozzie Ostrich, and I run the best bird

tour company in the whole feathered world. Birds

flock from the south, the north, and even the icy

_____ to ride in Ozzie's Balloons. My
1

guests today included a young _____
2

from Spain, her elderly _____, and
3

a purple _____ who was visiting
4

from Australia. We soared high above the

_____ and looked at the beautiful,
5

faraway _____. Then, one guest leaned
6

too far out of the _____ and nearly fell
7

overboard! He was a barnyard _____
8

who never learned to fly, so he wouldn't have

been able to fly to safety! Thinking fast, I thrust a

_____ in his direction. He grabbed on
9

with his _____ and I pulled him up into
10

the balloon! He was so grateful he gave me a big

_____. I put my wing around him and
11

we enjoyed the rest of the lovely _____
12

together. Just another day on the job.

Hidden Pictures®

Write a number below each object based on the order in which you find it
in the big picture. Then flip the page to create a silly story with the objects!

bell

( )

pencil

( )

ice-cream cone

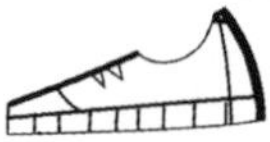

( )

sneaker

( )

spoon

( )

crescent moon

( )

megaphone

( )

leaf

( )

paper clip

( )

comb

( )

egg

( )

toothbrush

( )

BONUS
Can you also find these objects?

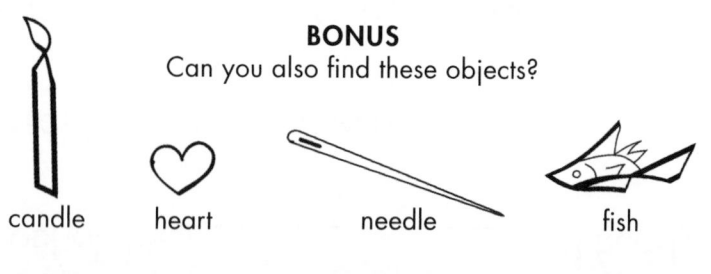

candle   heart   needle   fish

Jump In!

Flip the page!

Jump In!

Write the object names in the numbered spaces. For example, if you found the egg first, write "egg" in the first blank.

Introducing the Kanga-Jump 5000! This fancy

_____ is guaranteed to make the
　　　　1

kangaroos in your life happier than a frog on a

bouncy _____. If you thought your
　　　　　　　2

kangaroo could leap high before, wait until you see

what happens when her _____ hits this
　　　　　　　　　　　　3

ultra-trampoline. The Kanga-Jump 5000 features a

genuine leather _____, a shiny steel
　　　　　　　　　　　4

_____, and a nice _____
　　　5　　　　　　　　　　　　　　　　　6

to make fur flap in the breeze. But don't just take

our word for it. Here is what our customer Mr.

_____ had to say: "Last week, I bought
        7

the Kanga-Jump 5000 for my _____.
                                        8

She loves it! She won't even jump off to eat her

favorite meal, _____ and cheese! I
                        9

recommend this with all my _____."
                                    10

So there you have it. Our awesome Kanga-Jump

5000 is the best _____ in the business.
                        11

We guarantee you'll love it—or we'll give you your

_____ back!
        12

Hidden Pictures®

Write a number below each object based on the order in which you find it in the big picture. Then flip the page to create a silly story with the objects!

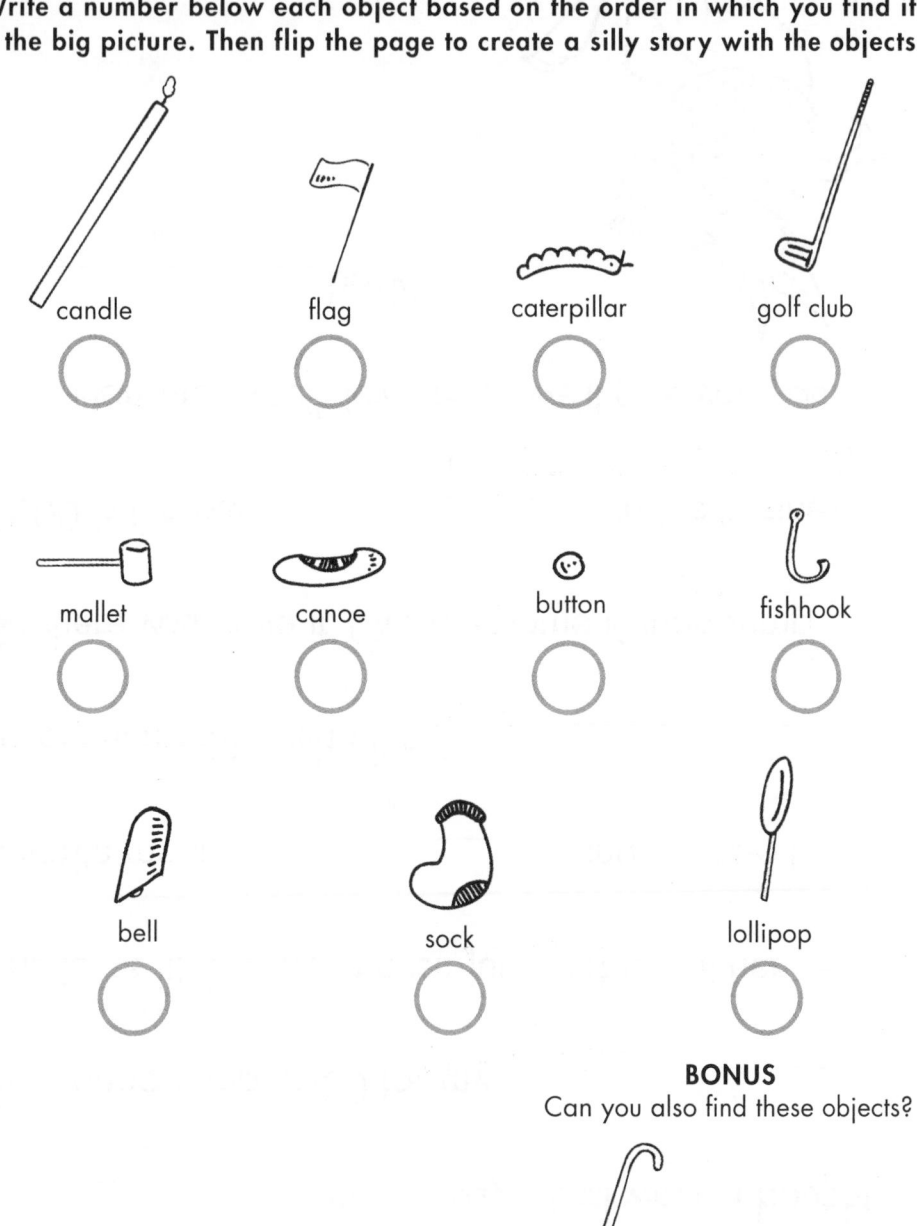

candle

flag

caterpillar

golf club

mallet

canoe

button

fishhook

bell

sock

lollipop

BONUS
Can you also find these objects?

cane

snake

Top Hog

PIG OF THE YEAR!

Illustrated by Ron Lieser

Flip the page!

Top Hog

Write the object names in the numbered spaces. For example, if you found the button first, write "button" in the first blank.

It is with great pleasure that I accept the title

"Pig of the Year." My grandfather, Swinegustus

_____ Hog, once held this honor. I am
_____1_____

proud to follow him. Friends, I like to eat the last

piece of _____ in the trough, I like to
_____2_____

roll in _____-scented mud, and I love a
_____3_____

good _____ in the morning. But there is
_____4_____

nothing I like more than winning this honor. So I vow

to put more _____ in each of our bellies,
_____5_____

to cover the _____ with more mud
_____6_____

(You can never have too much mud, can you?), and

to build the best _____ our farm has
7

ever seen. I will make this year the best that it can be.

Remember my slogan, "An extra _____
8

in our troughs! Another _____ in our
9

stalls!" I promise this to every pig in this farm, or

my name is not _____ X. Hambone.
10

Thanks to each and every _____ in the
11

audience!

Hidden Pictures®

Write a number below each object based on the order in which you find it in the big picture. Then flip the page to create a silly story with the objects!

doughnut

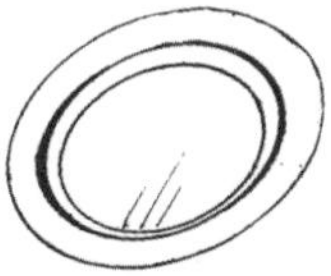

◯

plate

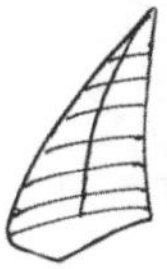

◯

sailboat

◯

pencil

◯

spoon

◯

party hat

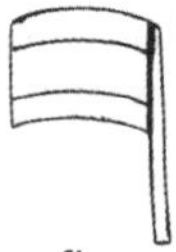

◯

flag

◯

tennis ball

◯

raindrop

◯

magnet

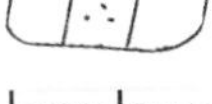

◯

bandage

◯

candle

◯

BONUS
Can you also find these objects?

handbell

egg

The Mane Event

Illustrated by Rocky Fuller

Flip the page!

The Mane Event

Write the object names in the numbered spaces. For example, if you found the magnet first, write "magnet" in the first blank.

Mr. Lion, also known as Mr. Fancy

_____, was ready for a haircut. And not

1

just any cut. He wanted a _____ that

2

would make his friends say, "Oh my, he looks like a

new _____!" There's only one place to

3

go for a cut like that: Hair Today, _____

4

Tomorrow, the shop on First Street. Mr. Lion knew

what he wanted: a long _____ in

5

the front, a short _____ in the back,

6

and one curly _____ on each side.

7

Piccadilly Peacock set to work. She's the best in the business. First she lathered his mane with the finest

liquid _____. Then she sharpened
8

her _____ and began snipping.
9

Fast and furious flew the hairs from Mr. Lion's

_____. Almost every inch of the floor was
10

covered in hair. After a quick brush and blow dry, he

was gazing in the _____ at a brand new
11

_____. "Wow!" he said happily. "I look
12

grrrr-eat!"

Hidden Pictures®

Write a number below each object based on the order in which you find it in the big picture. Then flip the page to create a silly story with the objects!

sailboat

thermometer

banana

boot

bowl

snail

teacup

pear

fish

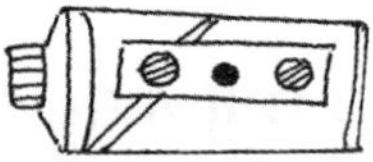

toothpaste

button

butterfly

BONUS
Can you find these objects?

needle

heart

Pig Ballet

Illustrated by Diana Zourelias

Flip the page!

Pig Ballet

Write the object names in the numbered spaces. For example, if you found the banana first, write "banana" in the first blank.

Did you know that pigs make great ballerinas? I saw

proof with my own eyes. After my _____

1

class today, I put on my _____, dusted

2

off my _____, and headed for the

3

door. That's when I peeked in a _____

4

and noticed another class going on. The room was

filled with pigs! And each pig was wearing a fluffy

pink _____. Music was blasting, and

5

the _____ in charge was tapping her

6

hoof and calling out instructions. "Don't raise your

_____ too high, dear!" she'd say, and
                7

"Remember to swing your _____ in
                                  8

the air and leap over the _____!" Pigs
                                    9

were leaping and twirling and prancing across the

polished _____. All of a sudden, one
              10

took a tumble. Another rushed over, offered her a

_____, and helped her up. Then they
          11

kept dancing, arms around each other. I pinched

myself to make sure it wasn't all a _____.
                                              12

It wasn't. Pigs aren't just great ballerinas; they also

make good friends.

Hidden Pictures®

Write a number below each object based on the order in which you find it in the big picture. Then flip the page to create a silly story with the objects!

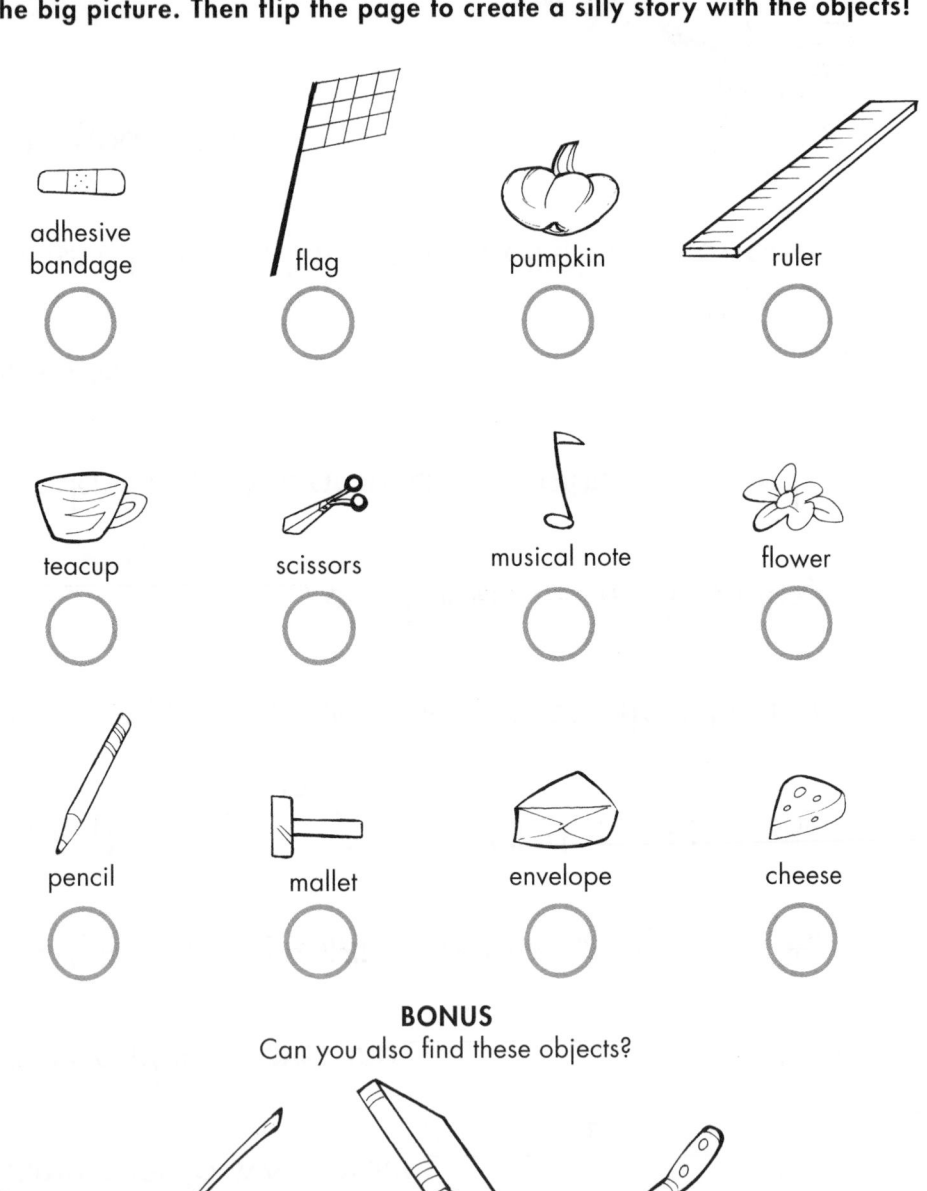

adhesive
bandage

flag

pumpkin

ruler

teacup

scissors

musical note

flower

pencil

mallet

envelope

cheese

BONUS
Can you also find these objects?

needle

book

butter knife

Splash!

Illustrated by Rocky Fuller

Flip the page!

Splash!

Write the object names in the numbered spaces. For example, if you found the pumpkin first, write "pumpkin" in the first blank.

It was the day of the big swim meet. Every

_____ in town was there to cheer
      1

on the team. I was wearing my lucky waterproof

_____ and brand-new goggles. When
      2

the _____ sounded, I dove in as fast as
        3

I could. Even underwater I could hear my Great-Aunt

_____ cheering for me. My family gets
      4

really excited about every single _____ I'm
                           5

in. Last race, my dad stood up and screamed, "You can

do it, my little _____ !"
           6

I love my dad to pieces, but I was embarrassed as a

turtle out of its _____ . Today, as my

7

_____ popped out of the water, I heard my

8

mom yell, "Good job, my sweet _____!"

9

My _____ turned bright red, but I put

10

my head under the water and kept on swimming as

fast as my _____ would go. And when

11

I reached the _____ first, I leapt into my

12

family's arms for a hug.

Hidden Pictures®

Write a number below each object based on the order in which you find it in the big picture. Then flip the page to create a silly story with the objects!

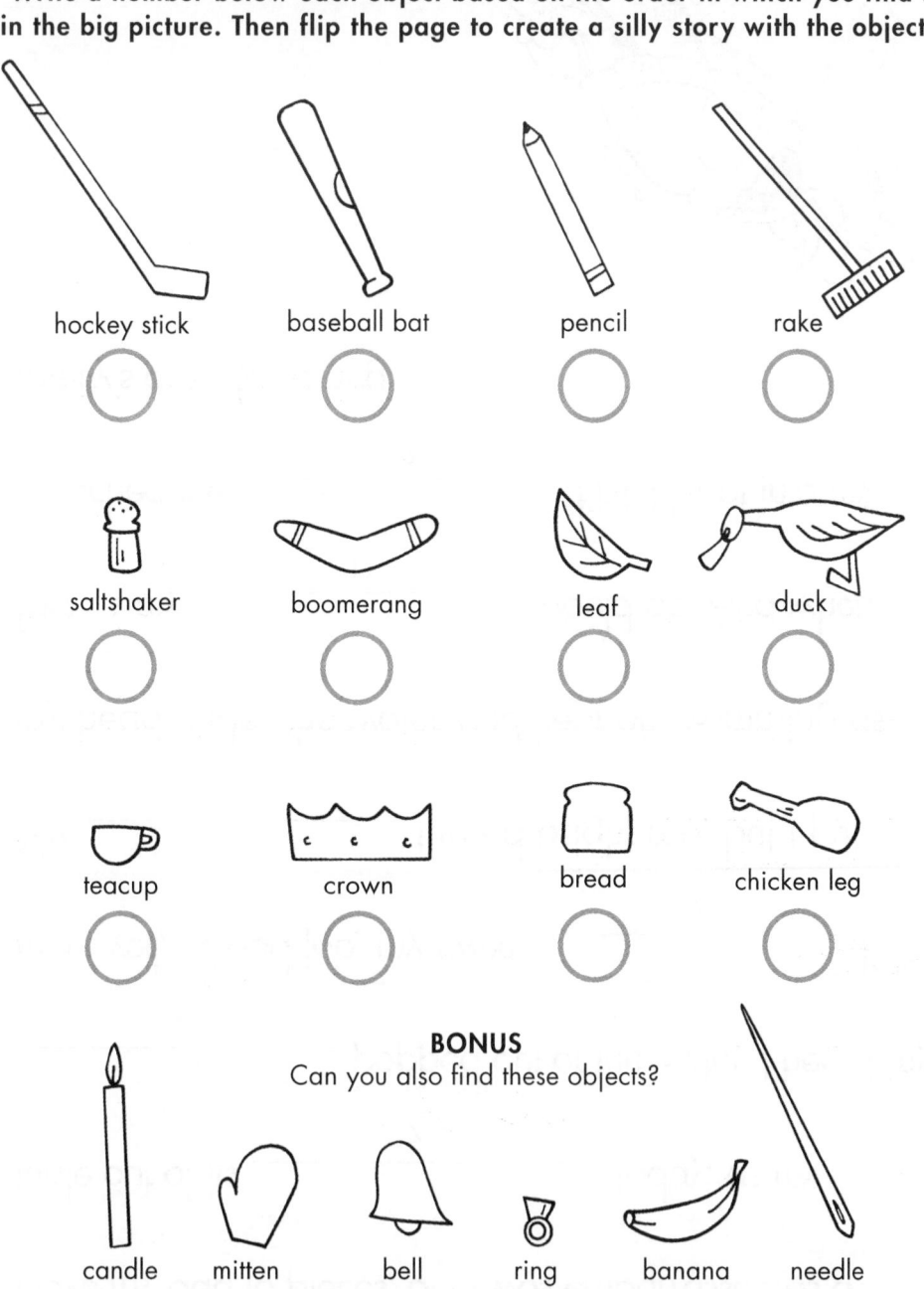

hockey stick

baseball bat

pencil

rake

saltshaker

boomerang

leaf

duck

teacup

crown

bread

chicken leg

BONUS
Can you also find these objects?

candle   mitten   bell   ring   banana   needle

Neck to Neck

Illustrated by Mike DeSantis

Flip the page!

Neck to Neck

Write the object names in the numbered spaces. For example, if you found the pencil first, write "pencil" in the first blank.

Here at the Big and Tall _____ Shop,
1

we can find a necktie for any _____.
2

If your neck is taller than a _____
3

on an extension ladder, no problem! If your neck

is wider than a whale that swallowed a jumbo

_____, no worries! We will find the
4

perfect tie. Our selection can't be beat. We have

ties with neon _____ patterns, ones
5

made of the finest _____ silk, and you'll
6

just love our many ties from the famous designer

Madam _____! They are as soft as a
                7

fuzzy _____. Today at the shop, we
              8

pleased three very tall and very fussy individuals.

One of them said he could only wear a tie with a

smiling _____ on it. We searched on
                9

every _____ in the store but couldn't
              10

find it. But then the customer spied it on the highest

_____ in the far corner. It helps to be tall
        11

sometimes! We put the tie on him, and he said it fit like

a _____. Another satisfied customer!
        12

Hidden Pictures®

Write a number below each object based on the order in which you find it in the big picture. Then flip the page to create a silly story with the objects!

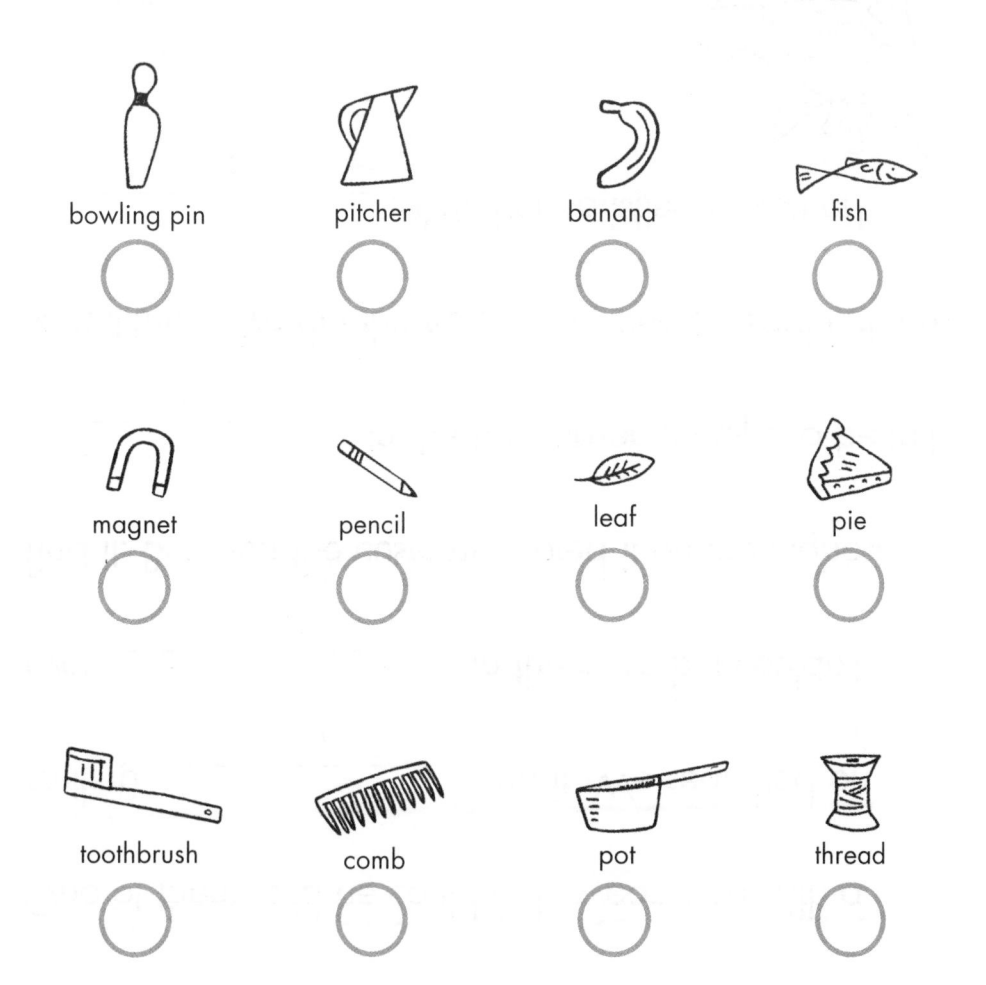

bowling pin

pitcher

banana

fish

magnet

pencil

leaf

pie

toothbrush

comb

pot

thread

Hop To It

Illustrated by Dave Klug

Flip the page!

Hop To It

Write the object names in the numbered spaces. For example, if you found the pie first, write "pie" in the first blank.

Have you ever seen a frog jump as high as a

_____? I did! Today was the big

1

race at the fair. I entered my _____,

2

Matilda, in the competition. At first, I wasn't sure if

she knew where the starting _____

3

was. But when the _____ sounded,

4

she put her _____ in the right direction

5

and hopped down the path as fast as her springy

_____ could carry her. I was as proud

6

as a _____. "Go, Matilda!" I cheered.

7

But then something happened. Matilda looked at the

_____ next to her. Then she leapfrogged
8

right over him and out onto the _____.
9

The other frog followed her with a leap that seemed

as tall as a two-story _____. The crowd
10

gasped. "_____!" I exclaimed. In the
11

end, the third frog won the race. But Matilda had

made a friend. That's what I call a "ribbitting" good

_____!
12

Hidden Pictures®

Write a number below each object based on the order in which you find it in the big picture. Then flip the page to create a silly story with the objects!

mushroom ◯

pizza ◯

game piece ◯

fish ◯

hammer ◯

bell ◯

spoon ◯

pencil ◯

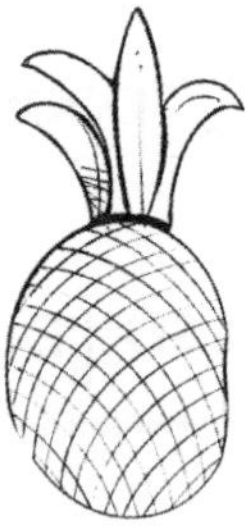

pineapple ◯

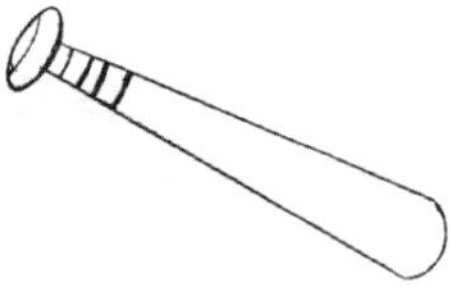

baseball bat ◯

flag ◯

arrow ◯

BONUS
Can you also find these objects?

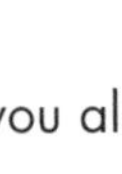

heart

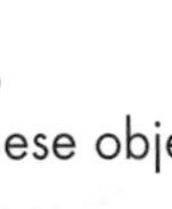

butterfly

The Big Slurp

Flip the page!

The Big Slurp

Write the object names in the numbered spaces. For example, if you found the pineapple first, write "pineapple" in the first blank.

Today was my best friend's birthday. I was thrilled

when she told me her party was at the local

_____ shop. They serve all kinds of
1

delicious ice cream there: Blue _____,
2

Chunky Almond _____, and her favorite
3

flavor, White _____ Crunch. Instead of
4

serving a chocolate _____ with candles,
5

she ordered a giant mug filled with eight scoops of

_____ and topped with a mound of
6

whipped _____. The treat was so big,
7

she couldn't possibly eat it all. So we all shared it. I've

never tasted a more delicious _____ in
                                            8

my entire life! It was rich and creamy and had just a

hint of _____. I could have slurped it all
                  9

day long. But then we all started feeling full. I just had

to put my _____ down. My friend finally
                  10

managed to scoop up the last couple of bites with

her _____. Then we all sang "Happy
            11

_____ to You!" It was the perfect party.
          12

Answers

Page 1

There are 2 carrots and 6 bananas.
There are more bananas.

snail: page 43

bat: page 23

duck: page 51

caterpillar: page 35

butterfly: page 15

3 Kitten Cuddles

7 Big Fish

11 Bug Band

15 Monkeyshines

19 Surf's Up!

23 Bunny Bakery

27 Bird's-Eye View

31 Jump In!

35 Top Hog

39 The Mane Event

43 Pig Ballet

Answers

47 Splash!

51 Neck to Neck

59 The Big Slurp

55 Hop To It